LEXINGTON AND CONCORD, 1775
WHAT REALLY HAPPENED

Powder horn carried by Edmund Bancroft, Pepperell minuteman
on April 19, 1775.

Lexington and Concord, 1775

What Really Happened

by JEAN POINDEXTER COLBY

Illustrated with Photographs by Barbara Cooney
Old Prints and Maps

HASTINGS HOUSE • *Publishers*

NEW YORK

Library of Congress Cataloging in Publication Data

Colby, Jean Poindexter, 1908–
    Lexington and Concord, 1775: what really happened.

    SUMMARY: Examines what happened before, during, and
after the first battles of the American Revolution and
provides a tour through the sites that witnessed these
events.
    Bibliography: p.
    1. Lexington, Battle of, 1775 — Juvenile literature.
2. Concord, Battle of, 1775 — Juvenile literature.
[1. Lexington, Battle of, 1775. 2. Concord, Battle of,
1775. 3. United States — History — Revolution, 1775–
1783] I. Cooney, Barbara, 1917–   illus. II. Title.
E241.L6C67   973.3'311   74-11466
ISBN 0-8038-4292-9

Published simultaneously in Canada by
Saunders of Toronto, Ltd., Don Mills, Ontario

Printed in the United States of America

Contents

The battle on Concord Bridge, an engraving by W. J. Edwards from a painting by Alonzo Chappel.

Introduction

Our American Revolution is only one of many that have taken place over the world. It was followed by the French Revolution, the Russian Revolution and many others, but strangely enough, it was one of the few anywhere whose purpose was to return to the old form of government. The original charters had given the colonies practically home rule, and when Parliament revoked them and also the right of colonial assemblies to agree or disagree to taxes affecting them, trouble began. (More about this may be found in Part I.)

Another unusual thing about the American Revolution was its start. Not that there is a prescribed way to start a revolution, but it is customary to have more activity on a grand scale preceding it, and more people milling around dead set against the ruling powers than was the case at Lexington and Concord. For instance, one could truthfully say that at dawn on April 19, 1775, many colonists in America did not seriously consider being separated from the mother country. The Massachusetts rebels and other groups like them were an exception, and even as the minutemen were assembling at Concord, diplomats like Benjamin Franklin were preparing to meet with British leaders to arbitrate the difficulties.

So the action at Lexington and Concord was a little precipitate, and not very impressive in size, either. The

English quickly played it down while the rebel leaders played it up, and for years historians debated whether it really *was* the start of the Revolution, or just the regional prelude, so to speak, for the national orchestration to come.

Consequently, in history books, the assessment of the fighting at Lexington and Concord has varied. In the nineteenth century many accounts were inflated by ancestor-worship, or they exaggerated the action into melodrama as if to give it stature. The twentieth century has established its significance as new, original source material has come to light, and as realization dawned that such a low-key start was more typical of America than anything grandiose would have been.

Anyway, for two hundred years, the subject has been good for an argument that has never been dropped. There have been thousands of articles, monographs, orations, sermons, books, and chapters in books about it. It has provided inspiration for songs, plays, musical comedies, operas, poetry and novels, and a researcher could literally spend his life reading what has been written about it.

Part IV of this book attempts to summarize these multitudinous literary efforts, and makes it plain that my purpose in adding another volume to the overwhelming number on the subject is to get down to the basic facts, consider again the accounts of the men who were there on the spot, and describe briefly but clearly the events of that long day for those who are approaching them for the first time.

The reader can then evaluate these events on his own, perhaps reassessing some factors that might have been a little neglected in the scholarly evaluation and re-evaluation.

Take, for instance, the weather. It is proven beyond a doubt that April 19, 1775 was a beautiful spring day. Now, born-and-bred New Englanders know that such days are rare, especially in April. It is traditional for students in New England to throw academic shackles to the wind and boil over with high spirits on such a day. Even older people are apt to say, "It's too nice to stay indoors and work."

Of course, many colonists had built up tremendous resentment over the years, and had kept their muskets oiled and hung over the fireplace for a long time before that date, but it took beautiful weather and the march of a few hundred British soldiers for them to reach up for their guns and step purposefully out the door even though they knew they might never return. To put it simply, April 19, 1775 was a good day to start a revolution. Here is how it happened.

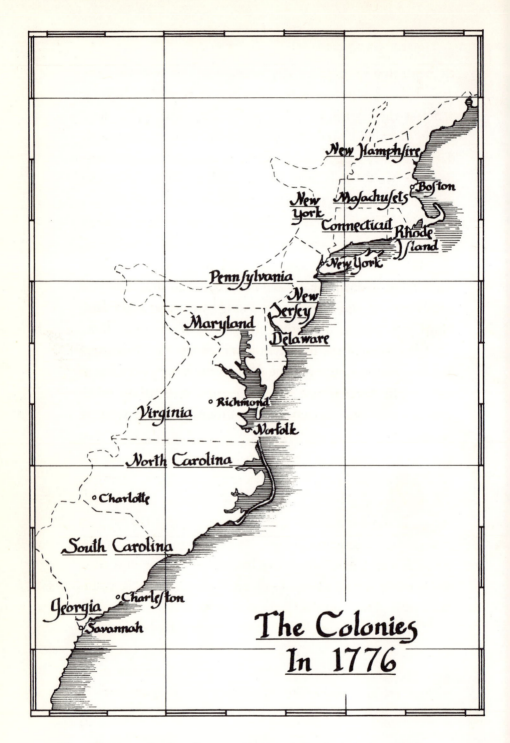

New Hampshire

Boston

New York   Massachusets

Connecticut   Rhode Island

New York

Pennsylvania

New Jersey

Maryland   Delaware

Virginia

Richmond

Norfolk

North Carolina

Charlotte

South Carolina

Georgia   Charleston

Savannah

The Colonies
In 1776

The thirteen colonies. Crown charters defined their boundaries
and allowed indefinite westward expansion. This map shows the
extent of settlement in 1775.

PART ONE

Colonial America Before the Revolution Started

In 1760 there were 13 colonies in North America, all of them under English rule, and all on the east coast. Behind them toward the west was wilderness, its extent and character unknown, cut through only by rivers and Indian trails.

On some of the rivers and trails east of the Mississippi River were French trading posts and forts but no towns or cities. The French in Canada were the first to do much trading with the Indians, but for many years they were traders only — not settlers. They wanted the Indians' furs because they could sell them at a high price in Europe; the profits from such transactions were tremendous. Soon the English went after these furs and also the Indian territories, as did the French when they saw the growing success of the American colonies. So the conflict between the English and French over the Indians' fur trade and their lands could not be avoided, especially as the mother countries were at war on the European continent.

Hence the French and Indian War took place in this country while the Seven Years' War was being fought in Europe. English soldiers, aided by many American colonists, were able to capture the important French forts. It

was a long conflict, finally ended by the Treaty of Paris in 1763, which gave Canada to England.

The French and Indian War was over years before the battle of Lexington and Concord, but that war was really the start of trouble between England and its American colonies, even though many Americans had fought shoulder to shoulder with Englishmen against France and its Indian allies. The difficulty was that the cost of the war had been high, and the English king, George III, felt that the Americans should help pay for it. After all, the money had been spent defending their colonies.

The Americans, especially the radicals in Boston, thought differently. These included Sam Adams, a fiery man in his forties who was an unsuccessful businessman but became a leader of the agitators against Britain, and eventually a foremost patriot and member of the Massachusetts Provincial Congress;* John Hancock, who inherited great wealth and a prominent position in Boston, attended Harvard College, and also became known as a revolutionary leader and a member of the Congress; Dr. Joseph Warren, another Harvard graduate and a doctor who treated rich and poor alike (an unusual practice in those times) and gave up wealth and prominence to lead the patriots. He organized a most successful spy system against the British and was admired and revered by all.

* The King had done away with the General Courts, which had been the colonial government in Massachusetts, so the citizens formed the Massachusetts Provincial Congress, composed of delegates from all the towns. For more details, see page 36.

Samuel Adams by John Singleton Copley.

Above: Dr. Joseph Warren and Mrs. Warren. Left: John Hancock by John Singleton Copley. Facing page above: Home of the Warrens in Boston. Below: Hancock house on Beacon Hill, Boston.

Before 1760 the 13 colonies had not been taxed by the mother country except when their own assemblies had voted it, and they considered that the established system. Most Englishmen, on the other hand, believed that Parliament had a right to tax any part of the British Empire. This seemed only fair when taxes at home in England were so high and so far-reaching. For instance, there was even a tax on windows! Every Englishman who owned a house had to pay a certain amount for each window in his house or barn. Many were bricked up to avoid this tax, and some of these can be seen today, still closed.

In 1764 Parliament was very short of money and passed a good many "resolutions" or taxes that were to be collected in America. One of them was the Stamp Act. This called for a sum of money to be paid for every legal stamp put on printed documents like wills and deeds* — even on newspapers. The colonists had not agreed to this tax, and they objected violently, even though the money from it was to be spent in their country.

* It is interesting to note that we pay for similar stamps now on all legal documents.

Facsimile of a British tax stamp, 1765.

Colonists burn stamped paper to protest the Stamp Act. A German cartoon, 1764.

Tax collectors were not popular. In fact, many were rolled in tar and then in feathers when they tried to collect the money. Angry mobs walked the streets of many towns, calling out, "Taxation without representation is tyranny." They felt that men from the colonies should be sent to Parliament and have a vote before any taxes were passed affecting the colonies. George III and his Prime Minister, Lord North, thought this was a ridiculous demand. They had never been to America and did not try to understand how the colonists felt.

A lot of people here agreed with them. In all the important cities like Boston, New York, Philadelphia, Williamsburg and Savannah many men and their families were still loyal to the King. It was also true that there were many Englishmen who sided with the Americans, even some members of Parliament.

On this side of the Atlantic, the protests against the Stamp Act grew louder. In fact, this Act was responsible for the colonies getting together for the first time. In October 1765 each one except Georgia sent a representative to a meeting in New York City which was later called the

The *Pennsylvania Journal* illustrated its opposition to the Stamp Act with this skull and crossbones version of a British tax stamp.

The funeral of the Stamp Act. Chancellor of the Exchequer, George Grenville, bears the coffin while British ministers march in procession. A British cartoon.

Stamp Act or First Continental Congress.* There the colonials joined in a single formal protest to the King.

King George considered this "Congress" a bunch of insolent farmers and paid no attention. Parliament *did* repeal the Stamp Act in 1766, but the Townshend Acts, passed in 1767, were just as bad or worse. For one thing, they applied to Americans alone and put duties on all goods sent to America. These included glass, paper, paint and tea, items badly needed in the colonies.

* At this time there was no Congress or Senate in Washington — no central government at all. In fact there was no city of Washington.

The women of Edenton, North Carolina, signing a protest against the tax on tea. A British cartoon.

It is not hard to imagine how furious this made most Americans because it affected many of the daily necessities, as our sales tax does now. Both people who sold the goods and people who bought them suffered. The tax on tea was especially resented. Almost everyone drank tea.

Secret societies and some not so secret were formed all over the colonies to protest this new outrage. One group, the Sons of Liberty in Boston, rallied around their Liberty Tree as did other rebel groups around theirs. These trees originally grew in public squares that served as convenient meeting places for patriots in various towns. Boston's tree, a big elm, was finally cut down by British soldiers, but that did not stop the meetings, and the spot on the corner of Washington and Essex Streets where the tree stood is now

The Liberty Tree.

The Green Dragon Tavern in Boston, one of the meeting places of the Sons of Liberty.

marked by a plaque. At their meetings, Sam Adams, John Hancock, Dr. Joseph Warren, and other Sons of Liberty, were very good at rousing the Boston people to anger against England.

So many protest meetings were held that the Massachusetts Royal Governor fled to his country estate, and Boston was actually ruled by mobs. The governor had to ask Parliament for help, and regiments and artillery were sent down from Nova Scotia to restore order. These soldiers, patrolling the streets, were jeered at by townsfolk who called them "redcoats" or "lobster-backs" because of the color of their elegant red uniforms.*

* Elegant they were, practical they were not. Everything about them was tight: the tunic, the knee breeches, the high boots. Also, in accordance with the fashion of the day, foot soldiers as well as the officers wore their hair long and done up in a queue in back that was well-greased and then heavily powdered, as were their sideburns.

Above: Boston Common. People strolling, cows dozing and British troops drilling. From a water color by Christian Remick, 1768. Below: Landing of British troops, Boston Harbor, 1768. An engraving by Paul Revere.

This caused many small street fights, one of which resulted in the Boston Massacre on March 5th, 1769. It was hardly a massacre because only four rioters and one innocent boy were killed, but reports (probably written by Sam Adams) blew up the importance of the incident. Actually, the facts are that the sentries should not have fired

The Boston Massacre. An engraving by Paul Revere.

The Old State House, scene of the Boston Massacre.

George III.

The Lion and the Unicorn. Details from the Old State House.

on the mob, but they and the soldiers who came to their rescue were being tormented and might have been assaulted by the rapidly growing crowd.

It is also true that on the very day of the "massacre" the British Parliament repealed the Townshend Acts, keeping only the tax on tea. This appeased the objectors and there was no concentrated trouble until May 1773 when the East India Company was given the monopoly of the American tea trade. That meant that all the Americans who imported tea were cut out of business, and the shopkeepers who sold it had to stock only the East India Company's tea.

Faneuil Hall in Boston.

Again meetings of the Sons of Liberty were called, especially in seaports like Boston. There were great cries of outrage in Faneuil Hall* and other public places, but England turned a deaf ear to them. Three large ships loaded with tea set sail for Boston and docked there late in November. By law cargo had to be unloaded in 20 days, but the Sons of Liberty said they would tar and feather any seaman

* Pronounced *Fan-el* and named after its donor, Peter Faneuil, a wealthy Bostonian. It was built in 1742 with market stalls on the first floor and a large room for public meetings on the second. This building is still used for the same purpose today.

A New Method of MACARONY MAKING, as practised at BOSTON in NORTH AMERICA.

217

Printed for Carington Bowles, N°. 69 in S.t Pauls Church Yard, London.

Tarring and feathering — a threat to any seaman unloading tea in Boston Harbor.

who landed this tea. So the great chests remained on board even as the deadline for unloading, December 17th, came closer and closer.

On the night of December 16th, a large and rowdy gathering filled the Old South Meeting House. Three men talked with great fire and persuasion against English rule and laws: Sam Adams, John Hancock and Josiah Quincy, a lawyer who was later sent to England to plead the

A tea chest that survived the Boston Tea Party.

DESTRUCTION OF THE TEA IN BOSTON HARBOUR.

The Boston Tea Party.

patriots' cause. Suddenly during the meeting a signal was given. War whoops filled the air and about 150 men, waving tomahawks and dressed as Indians, poured into the street and down to the waterfront. Once on the tea ships, they demanded and got the keys from the guards, then ran below and hauled on deck the despised cargo. It was only a matter of minutes before the harbor was afloat with tea and tea crates. What a tea party! It was the most famous one ever held in the world.

* * *

Boston Harbor blockaded by the British fleet.

Many believe that this was the first act of the American Revolution. Certainly it aroused and unified the colonies. How brave and daring those Boston men seemed to the other colonists, to openly defy the King of England in this way!

Across the ocean it was a different matter. The King, Lord North, and Parliament took the act as an insult, and on June 1st, 1774, the port of Boston was closed by law as punishment. The redcoats took over the city and patrolled

32

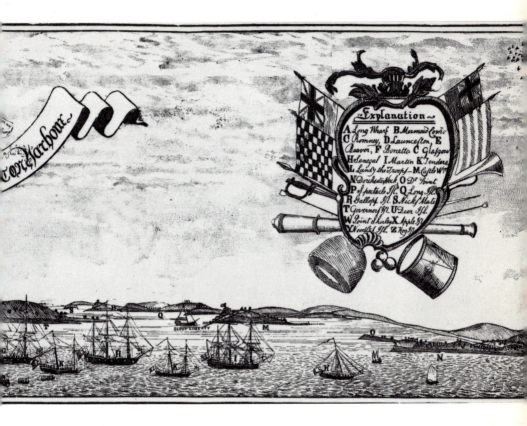

the waterfront so that no goods left or came into the wharves.

Naturally Boston suffered badly because it depended on its sea trade, but neighboring colonies helped out by sending food and other supplies over land routes. So the following winter was fairly peaceful — even to the point where the British officers frequently met with some of the Massachusetts leaders like John Hancock at dinners, dances and other social affairs.

British cartoon showing starving Bostonians hauled up the Liberty Tree, while neighboring towns come to their aid with food.

General Thomas Gage and
his headquarters in Boston.

Meanwhile General Thomas Gage had become Royal
Governor of the Massachusetts Bay Colony and Commander of all the British forces in America. His troops
had been increased in order to hold down the Boston rebels and numbered around 3000 men, one to every five
Bostonians. He exercised them often, sometimes marching
them in full battle array with bayonets gleaming and pen-
nants flying. This must have been to impress the colonists
as well as to keep the soldiers in condition.

Certainly the colonists kept track of every movement the British made. This was done at the order of the Committee of Safety. As has been said, the King had done away with the General Courts to keep Massachusetts from governing itself, but the citizens had formed the Massachusetts Provincial Congress, composed of delegates from all the towns. The Congress appointed this important, inner Committee of Safety to handle emergency decisions, and to watch the British day and night. Dr. Warren was in charge of the Boston espionage group.

The British also had a spy system. Word of rebel activities was brought to General Gage almost daily by one Dr. Benjamin Church*, a member of the Committee of Safety, but a traitor to the rebel cause. From him General Gage knew well that the colonists were piling up guns, ammunition and food stores outside of Boston. The biggest stockpile, he had heard, was in Concord.

* For more information on Church, see Part IV, page 91.

Unite or die. A cartoon that inspired several patriot battleflags.

PART TWO

The Night of April 18, 1775–
The British March
and the Rides of Paul Revere
and William Dawes

April 19, 1775–
The Battles of Lexington and
Concord, and the Retreat of the
British from Concord to Boston.

So the winter of 1774-1775 passed — each side watching the other. On the surface New Englanders were enjoying one of the mildest winters in years, and went about their usual cold weather chores, but General Gage knew there was trouble brewing. For instance, he had been observing with interest the stepped-up training of the local militia. These were small forces of men that each New England town had always kept ready in case of Indian attacks. Even in early Plimouth Plantation, every able male from young boys to old men had to serve so many days in the militia every year. He had to bring his musket to musters, their meetings for military training, or, if he did not

Musket used by Major John Buttrick at the North Bridge, Concord. It is 63½ inches long.

have one, he was supplied one from the town's military stores. The militia drilled on the town commons and were taught to prime and load their muskets. This had to be done every time the guns were fired, a lengthy process that allowed many an intended victim to get away. The muskets were also inaccurate at over a hundred yards distance, because they were smooth-bored, not rifled like later guns to spin the bullet, which kept it straight in flight. This explains the relatively low casualty rate during the Lexington and Concord fighting.

As the possibility of actual conflict with the British grew, the younger, able men of each village were put into a separate group and given a new name — minutemen. When warning came of a possible attack in their vicinity, these men were to be ready, guns in hand, in a matter of minutes. The boys and older men would stay home to guard the town itself while the minutemen marched off to report where needed. Although they had no uniforms, and did not look like soldiers, they were well organized and alert. The common belief is incorrect that the minutemen were country bumpkins who snatched up their guns, knew nothing of military strategy, and had no training. In fact, some of the leaders had fought in Europe, or with the British at Louisburg or Quebec during the French and Indian War.

Unlike the English, whose officers were noblemen who had bought their rank, each group of militia elected officers from their own company. This made for more unity and fellow-feeling. Regular meetings of these officers were held with those from nearby towns to plan mutual defense and to arrange for messengers on horseback, called *couriers*, or *expresses*, to ride between the towns. They were to spread any alarm.

Contents of a minuteman's buckskin hunting bag. Counterclock-wise from center: tiny horn for measuring gun powder, large powder horn, smaller powder horn containing finer powder for the flash pan, linen patches in tinder box, flints to strike sparks on the steel striker.

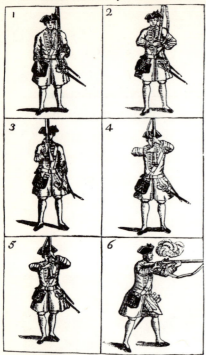

1 Take Care.   2 Join your Right-Hand to your Firelock.   3 Poife your Firelock.
4 Join your Left-Hand to your Firelock,   5 Cock your Firelock,   6 Prefent. Fire.

7. Recover your Arms. *See Fig.* 12.   Halfcock your Firelock.   8. Handle your
Primer.   9. Prime, *the firft Motion.*   10. Prime, *the laft Motion.*   11. Shut your
Pan.   12. Caft about to charge, *the firft Motion.*

13 Caft about to charge.   14 Handle your Cartridge.   15 Open your Cartridge
16 Charge with Cartridge.   17 Draw your Rammer, *the firft Motion.*   18 Draw
your Rammer, *the laft Motion.*

19 Shorten your Rammer, *the firft Motion.*   20 Shorten your Rammer.   21 Put
them in the Barrel.   22 Ram down your Charge.   23 Recover your Rammer
Shorten your Rammer. *See Fig.* 19.   24 Return your Rammer.

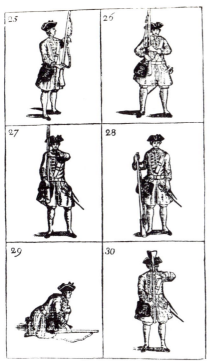

25. Caſt off your Firelock. *See Fig. 13.* Your right Hand under your Lock. 26. Poiſe. *See Fig. 2.* Shoulder. *See Fig. 1.* Reſt your Firelock 27. Order your Firelock, *the firſt Motion.* 28. Order your Firelock, *the laſt Motion.* 29. Ground your Firelock. Take up your Firelock. *See Fig. 28.* 30. Reſt. *See Fig. 26.* Club your Firelock, *the firſt Motion.*

31. Club your Firelock, *the third Motion.* 32. Club your Firelock, *the laſt Motion.* 33. Reſt. *See Fig. 26.* Secure your Firelock. 34. Shoulder. *See Fig. 1.* Poiſe. *See Fig. 3.* Reſt on your Arms. 35. Draw your Bayonet, *the firſt Motion.* 36. Draw your Bayonet.

37 Fix your Bayonet. 38 Reſt your Bayonet. 39 Charge your Bayonet Breaſt-high, *the ſecond Motion.* 40 Charge your Bayonet Breaſt-high. 41 Puſh your Bayonet. 42 Recover your Bayonet.

43 Reſt your Bayonet on your Left Arm. 44 Reſt, *fee Fig. 26.* Shoulder, *fee Fig. 1.* Preſent your Arms. 45 To the Right 4 Times. 46 To the Right about. 47 To the reſt as you were, *fee Fig. 44.* To the Left 4 Times. 48 To the Left about, *fee Fig. 46.* To the Right as you were, *fee Fig. 3.* Reſt on your Arms, *fee Fig. 34.* Unfix your Bayonet. Return your Bayonet, *fee Fig. 35.* Poiſe, *fee Fig. 3.* Shoulder, *fee Fig. 1.*

Manual of arms used by the minutemen and the militia.

Also, the colonial method of fighting was different from the British line-by-line attack in close formation over an open plain. From their earliest days the Americans had to fight over mountainsides and other rough ground, and had learned to hide behind trees, boulders or stonewalls while they took the time to prime and load their guns. The British method was to advance on the enemy in compact squares of marching men. The front line loaded, dropped to one knee and fired. Their places were taken by the second line who aimed and fired while the first line moved to the rear and reloaded. This was the usual European procedure and worked well if the enemy used the same tactics. The Lexington and Concord fight could be called the first battle where "guerrilla" or modern-type warfare was used during which men concealed themselves behind trees, walls, barns or anything handy, and constantly changed their position.

So, all over New England in the 1700's, these bands of informal soldiers were training. They were good fighters, but they often considered their family and farm obligations more important than their military service. During the Revolution, George Washington had great trouble with soldiers who would lay down their arms and go home when their enlistment period was over even though the situation was critical. The American Revolution was almost lost for that reason.

However, after the Boston Tea Party and the many hardships caused by the occupation of Boston by English soldiers, the spirit of the minutemen was high and united against England. They were ready for action, and in late

March the rebel leaders in Boston suspected that they would get it.

It was obvious that the British were up to something. The redcoats and Royal Marines were drilled more often, the horses exercised, and equipment and stores stacked in various places. The rebel leaders were so carefully watched that Sam Adams and John Hancock had already left for Lexington to escape possible capture by General Gage. But Dr. Warren remained in town along with two couriers, Paul Revere, a silversmith and ardent patriot, and William Dawes, a canny young smuggler. He had done well getting goods through the British lines after the port of Boston was closed, sometimes as a peddler, often as a friendly drunk. Soon he was to get *himself* through these lines.

Sunday, April 16th, Revere was sent by Dr. Warren to Lexington to warn Adams and Hancock that the British were planning some move. Warren suspected they were going after the rebel leaders but were also interested in the stores of ammunition and flour piled in Concord. He would send Revere to tell Hancock and Adams the exact route of the British march when he knew it.

Evidently General Gage felt assured that his plans to capture the stores were still secret, for Revere apparently had a pleasant horseback ride out to Lexington that Sunday through the spring countryside. None of the British patrols questioned him, but his news of the possible march startled the leaders in Lexington, and Hancock immediately sent a messenger to Concord with instructions to divide and move the stores. He also sent warnings to other towns that their minutemen should be ready for action, and soon.

Paul Revere, silversmith.

On Revere's return to Boston, he stopped in to see William Conant, colonel of the local militia, and told him that if the British marched he would alert him before he rode to Lexington and Concord to spread the alarm. They discussed which of the two routes out of Boston the British would take: "by land" over Boston Neck (at that time

Paul Revere's house.

Map of Boston, 1775, showing Boston Neck, the Charles River and Cambridge.

Boston was practically an island, connected to the mainland only by the Neck, now Roxbury), or "by sea," which meant transporting the troops on flat boats across the Charles River to Cambridge. This was much the shorter route to Lexington and Concord. They agreed that Conant was to look for a signal hung in the belfry of Christ Church (now called the Old North Church). The sexton, Robert Newman, was to hang one lantern if the British were leaving "by land" and two if "by sea." Either way Conant was to meet Revere with a horse to carry him to Lexington and then on to Concord.

Two days later, on April 18th, as soon as it was dark, General Gage marched seven or eight hundred of his men

46

in battle dress to the foot of Boston Common, which was then on the Charles River. These included nine regiments, each consisting of regular foot soldiers and light infantry. The latter were used as flankers because they were young and bold and could run along the sides of the road in front of the regular soldiers, clearing out obstacles, human and otherwise. There was also a company of grenadiers, all tall men and known for their strength, a contingent of Royal Marines, and one of Royal Welsh Fusiliers,* who had a goat with gilded horns as a mascot.

Several young officers in these companies were to write important descriptions of the next day's action. (See PART IV). Good examples are Lieutenant John Barker and Captain W. G. Evelyn of the King's Own Regiment, Ensigns Henry de Berniere and Jeremy Lister of the Tenth Lincolnshires, Lieutenant William Sutherland of the 38th South Staffordshires, and especially Lieutenant Frederick Mackenzie of the Royal Welsh Fusiliers.

Flatboats to ferry them across were made ready. The secret of the move supposedly was picked up by a young stableman who listened to some British officers talking about it as he groomed their horses. Some say a gunsmith heard of it and alerted Dr. Warren. At any rate, Warren immediately sent for Dawes and Revere, who informed Robert Newman at the North Church of the fact that the British were going "by sea." By that time it was dark, and soon two signal lanterns shone brightly from Christ Church steeple high over Boston town.

* British regiments were named after their commanding officers until the reign of George II, who started the policy of numbering them. After his death, however, they were called by the names of the districts or counties they came from.

One of the lanterns hung
in the belfry of the Old
North Church on the night
of April 18, 1775.

Dawes, as instructed, started out over the Neck, while
Revere had to make the perilous trip across the river to
Charlestown where his horse was waiting for him. It *was*
a perilous trip because the 64 gun British man-of-war, the
Somerset, was anchored right in the middle of the river
with a round-the-clock watch to stop anyone from cross-
ing in any kind of boat. Furthermore, it was bright moon-
light and very still. The sound of oars dipping in and out
of the water could carry far on such a night. But — so the
story goes — a girl friend in Boston had loaned Revere and
his companions, whose names are unknown, a petticoat to

The Old North Church.

muffle their oars. Anyway, Revere made the trip silently and safely. Here is his own description of it:

> I then went home, took my boots and surtout [coat], went to the north part of the town where I kept a boat; two friends rowed me across the Charles River, a little eastward where the Somerset man-of-war lay. It was then young flood, the ship was winding, and the moon was rising. They landed me on the Charlestown side.[1]

He was met on the opposite shore by Colonel Conant who had seen the lanterns and had brought him a "goode horse" borrowed from Deacon Larkin. That he was indeed "goode" was recognized by the British later on. Unfortunately nameless, he was to become one of the most famous animals in United States history, but no one knew it as he cantered down the road with his rider toward Lexington.*

Meanwhile, on the other side of town, Dawes, a truly daring young man, talked his way through the British patrol on the Neck by pretending he was a drunken young farmer on the way home after celebrating a successful day of trading in Boston with a pint or two of strong ale. Once through the patrols he too galloped toward Lexington.

Revere had started his ride at the same time, but was almost caught by two advance British guards who were standing in the shadow of a tree by a small marsh. However, the one who pursued Revere got bogged down in the swamp and Revere escaped. He rode swiftly to Menotomy

---

* There was another animal on the patriot side that night, too — a dog on the river shore who seemed to resent the Britishers' silent departure and barked. He was run through by a bayonet. (A British officer reported this incident in a letter.)

William Dawes.

(now Arlington) where he woke up the captain of the militia. He then galloped on to Lexington, arousing the inmates of each farmhouse along the way. Dawes did the same thing on his route.*

Revere reached Lexington in time to warn Hancock and Adams at the Reverend Jonas Clarke's house. Dawes soon appeared, and he and Revere started toward Concord to spread the alarm there. Along the way they were joined

* By this spreading of the alarm during the night, word passed swiftly from town to town all the way south to Rhode Island and Connecticut and north to New Hampshire. As a result farmers left their plows in the fields and tradesmen hurriedly locked their shops to join the groups of minutemen that poured into Concord all day long. Their growing numbers were an important factor in the events of the next 24 hours.

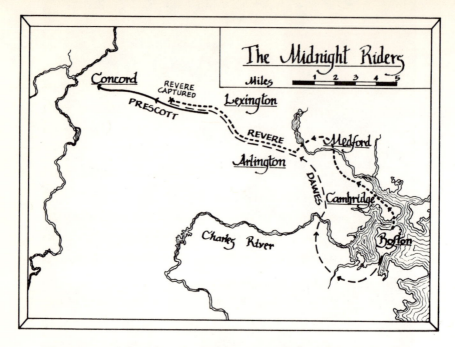

The routes of Paul Revere, William Dawes and Samuel Prescott.

by a Dr. Samuel Prescott, an enthusiastic patriot. He was on his way home to Concord after courting a girl in Lexington and was all too willing to help the cause. All three ran into an advance British patrol of young officers, but Prescott jumped his horse over a stone wall and escaped. Dawes managed to get away on foot but Revere was taken prisoner when he tried to ride off into nearby woods. When questioned about his purpose, he calmly told the truth. He was put with four other prisoners and taken along the road to Lexington until one of the officers decided he liked Revere's "goode" horse better than his own, and took it.** Revere took some rough treatment from his

** Deacon Larkin never got his horse back. For centuries people have wondered what happened to him. Some captured horses were shipped to England and continued their military life as mounts for officers serving in Europe. Few were killed. Horses were well taken care of by both sides.

guards after that, but was later released as the British considered him harmless and did not want to be bothered with guarding prisoners. He made his way back to Lexington but never did reach Concord.

Meanwhile, the captain of the Lexington militia, John Parker, hearing of the British march, had rounded up about 70 minutemen during the night. He did this to protect the safety of the citizens rather than with any thought of actual conflict. About 2 A.M. word came from poorly informed couriers that there was no sign of the British, so Captain Parker dismissed the men. Those living nearby went home; the others relaxed in a local public-house, Buckman's Tavern, on the green.

Buckman's Tavern, Lexington.

Toward dawn a horseman galloped madly in and told Parker that the British were at hand, as indeed they were — long columns of them on the outskirts of town. Parker immediately asked his 16-year-old drummer, William Diamond, to beat out the call to arms, and sent orders for his men to come back. However, only 30 or 40 had time to do

William Diamond's drum.

so before the clump of hundreds of boots could be heard, along with the rattle of swords and guns and the constant roll of drums. The rest of the militia were still running in as the sun came up, its first rays picking out the rows of splendid red uniforms advancing in marching formation on Lexington green. Here, on the edge of the grass, Parker, for some reason, had arranged his men in a long straggly line, presenting an easy target.

The first British regiment had just reached the meetinghouse when two or three officers (reports vary) rode up and reined their horses to a halt before Parker and his men.

54

None of them was Colonel Francis Smith, who was in charge of this expeditionary force. A fat, slow-moving, slow-thinking man, he had sent ahead his next-in-command, handsome Major John Pitcairn of the Royal Marines, one of the best-liked Britishers. Even the rebels in Boston during that long besieged winter had had a good word for him.

Looking over the roughly clad minutemen with their odd assortment of weapons, Pitcairn and his fellow officers were enraged to see even this token resistance to the royal command. Spurring his horse forward, he called out, "Ye villains, ye rebels, damn you, disperse!"

One of the other officers then shouted, "Lay down your arms! Damn you, why don't you lay down your arms?"

Pitcairn ordered his men to prime and load but not to fire. So did Captain Parker of the minutemen. His words have come down in history, although some authorities question them. "Don't fire unless fired upon but if they want a war, let it begin here!"

Then moments of indecision apparently followed. Pitcairn ordered his men to disarm the rebels but not to capture them. The men made no move to follow his orders, when suddenly a shot rang out. No one knows who fired it, but it is commonly believed to have been a Britisher although the official reports sent to England by the commanding officers claimed otherwise.

Paul Revere described the action as he saw it. He had returned to the Clarke house in Lexington after being released, in order to save a trunk of John Hancock's papers from falling into British hands.

Major Pitcairn and his troops disperse the rebels at Lexington Green. From an engraving by minuteman Amos Doolittle after a painting by his fellow soldier, Ralph Earle.

> We hurried toward Mr. Clarke's house. In our way we passed through the militia. There were about 50. When we had got about one hundred yards from the meeting house, the British troops appeared on both sides. In their front was an officer on horseback . . . I saw and heard a gun fired, which appeared to be a pistol . . . then a continual roar of musketry when we made off with the trunk.[2]

Pitcairn rode his horse up and down trying to stop the firing, but did not succeed until his superior, Colonel Smith, the commander, finally appeared. By that time eight of the Lexington militia lay dead; nine more were wounded. The British lost no men as apparently few shots were fired by the minutemen.

It took Pitcairn and Smith some time to quiet their men as they were very excited by their small victory. They finally reformed their ranks, however, gave their customary victory cheer, and marched down the road to Concord with fifes piping and drums beating.

Lexington was left to take care of the first dead and wounded of the American Revolution.

* * *

Meanwhile Dr. Prescott had reached Concord with the news of the British march, and Colonel James Barrett, in command of the regional militia, had ridden off to make sure the stores at his farm were well hidden. Major John Buttrick, his second in command, along with Captain Miles and Captain Brown of the two Concord companies, had rounded up about 250 minutemen, and decided to march them down the road to Lexington to meet the British. They were led by their own fifes and drums, sounding clear and true in the morning air. It was about 7 A.M. of a bright, sunny spring day.

Brass-tipped fife and carrying case used in the Revolutionary war.

Not far down the road, they heard the approaching British regiments and saw the long red line of uniformed men in the distance coming toward them. Major Buttrick, who had been given no orders to fire, waited until the two forces were about two hundred yards apart when he called "about-face." Whereupon his little force turned around and marched back to Concord. The enemy regiments followed them, keeping that exact distance. There were no yells of defiance and no shooting — just the two fife and drum corps tooting and pounding, sounding like a modern parade. As one minuteman, Corporal Amos Barrett, wrote later, "We had grande music!"

Once in the village the colonials gathered at their Liberty Pole in the center of town with about 150 new arrivals, but soon Major Buttrick and his officers decided to take their men over the North Bridge to higher ground on the other side of the Concord River. There they waited for the British.

The redcoats on arrival in Concord stacked their arms on the Common, and the officers sent to the Wright Tavern for breakfast. (This they paid for.) It was about 8 o'clock. Soon after some of the light infantry were sent south to guard a bridge there, while others followed the minutemen in the other direction toward the North Bridge. The grenadiers left in town began a very gentlemanly house-to-house search for weapons and supplies, which they confiscated. They also chopped up the Liberty Pole and some gun carriages and started a fire with them. At one point it blazed too high and an officer ordered them to douse it.

The British arrive in Concord. Major Pitcairn, with his spyglass, and Colonel Smith survey the scene from the Hill Burying Ground. In the background, a detachment destroys stores. Engraving by Amos Doolittle. Below: The same place today.

Actually, the billows of smoke from this dampened blaze were the real cause of the Concord battle. This is what happened. While the grenadiers were heaping wood on the fire in the village, part of the British light infantry had also crossed the North Bridge. To do this, their commander, Captain Lawrence Parsons, had had to lead his six companies right by the staring minutemen who were now stationed on a hill at the Buttrick farm some four hundred yards away on the other side. No one spoke a word. The Concord men just watched as about half of the Britishers took the road to the Barrett farm to look for stores of arms and shot supposed to be hidden there. Parsons left Captain Walter Laurie at the bridge with three English companies, part of which he stationed near it — the others on the low hills toward the town. The Britishers at the bridge eyed the minutemen up on the hill. The minutemen glared back but did not move down into firing range as they had been told not to shoot until ordered to do so.

Suddenly some of the patriots saw billows of smoke coming from the Common and mistook them for houses on fire. Whereupon Lieutenant Joseph Hosmer, an adjutant of the regional militia, called out, "Would ye let them burn down our town?"

Others shouted back, "No!"

So, quickly, the combined rebel forces, commanded by Major Buttrick and Captain Isaac Davis of the Acton militia, started to file down toward the bridge to recross it and return to rescue Concord.

The major ordered his men to load but not to fire. Seeing this action, the British light infantry on the hills moved down to join their fellows at the bridge. Now some 100 English soldiers faced about 400 minutemen, who were getting closer every minute.

At last the British Captain Laurie ordered his men to tear up the planking on the bridge so the Americans could not recross it. This they never did finish because warning shots from the British hit the water, and then all the redcoats fired a volley.

Isaac Davis and another Acton man were instantly killed. This so shocked Major Buttrick he forgot the usual military commands and shouted, "Fire, for God's sake, fire!"

The minutemen did. Three redcoats fell dead and ten or so were wounded. The rest turned and ran toward Concord in complete retreat. On the way they came upon

The battle on Concord Bridge, an engraving by W. J. Edwards from a painting by Alonzo Chappel.

North Bridge, Concord, today.

The engagement at the North Bridge, Concord. Engraving by Amos Doolittle based on a painting by Ralph Earle.

Colonel Smith, who had brought a company of grenadiers out to help them. Together they stumbled back to town under his protection. The minutemen crossed the bridge in pursuit, and took to a ridge directly above the road to the village to watch the rout. They left a small force at the bridge to care for their dead and wounded.

Soon Captain Parsons and his forces returned from the Barrett farm where they had found few stores of importance. It being spring, they took no note of a man plowing in a nearby field, turning up big furrows. Had they known that he was a rebel purposefully piling soil over colonial arms and other equipment, the story of the day might have been bloodier. As it was, the captain and his men walked back to the bridge, which they were allowed to cross without incident although the minutemen could easily have cut them off and taken all captive.

Wooden plough left in the field by Nathaniel Parker. Pepperell minuteman, when he answered the alarm on April 19, 1775.

The Bedford flag. Over 100 years old when carried by Bedford minutemen at the battle of Concord Bridge, this is the oldest existing flag in the United States.

Then followed several hours of strange inaction. The British troops reformed on the Common only to be disbanded in a matter of minutes. Smith had sent a messenger to General Gage early in the day asking for more troops. Perhaps he was waiting for them or resting his men, or perhaps he just could not make up his mind what to do. Finally, it was brought to his attention that the patriot forces were growing fast. Farmers from other towns had heard the news of the fighting and were hurrying by the hundreds to join their countrymen in Concord.

64

Meanwhile Major Buttrick and his men had breakfast of sorts — probably the townspeople watching the fight fed them what they could — and then moved to a hill overlooking the town. There they observed with fascination the forming and reforming of the British regiments. They were ready and waiting for any move.

It came about noon when the British columns regrouped again and started back down the Lexington Road to Boston. The light infantry trotted ahead and to the right and left as flankers. The grenadiers protected the walking wounded in the road while horses were supplied to the badly wounded. There was no fife and drum music — just the shuffle of weary feet.

Many of the flankers looted the houses as they passed but the retreat was orderly until the road narrowed at a bridge near Meriam's Corner and the British forces had to come together to pass over it. Then the minutemen, who

The Meriam house at Meriam's Corner, Concord.

The retreat of the British to Lexington. In the background Smith and Percy meet near burning houses. In the foreground, the rebels, sheltered by stone walls, fire on the British. Engraving by Amos Doolittle.

had followed closely, leaping from one sheltering building or wall to another, opened fire. It was not a professional volley — rather the guerrilla shoot-to-kill-when-you-can type of attack, described previously. The redcoats looked for a target to return fire but there was none. Each minuteman would load behind his particular protection, stick his head out quickly, aim at the crossed white straps on a scarlet tunic, fire, and duck back. Then he would reload and

repeat the process. When the ammunition of one company of militia gave out, another would take its place.

Fired upon from both sides, the redcoats must have found that six-mile walk back to Lexington a dreadful ordeal. The casualties were especially heavy at Job Brooks' house, where the road turned a corner, since known as the "Bloody Corner." Eight Britishers were killed and many wounded; three Americans died. Further down the

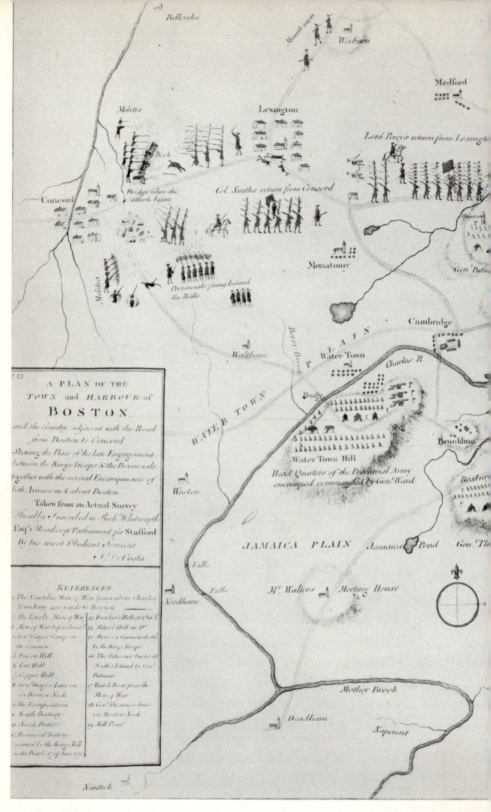

British picture map showing military action at Lexington and Concord

Upper left: first casualties on Lexington Common, confrontation at Concord's North Bridge. Top: British retreat to Boston.

Major John Pitcairn. The pistols Pitcairn lost in action at Concord.

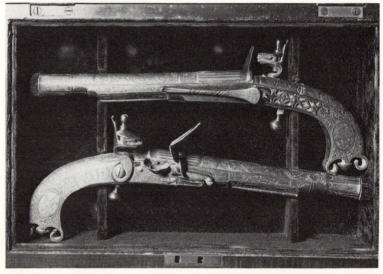

road at Fiske Hill, the redcoats began to panic, and Major Pitcairn rode up to try to organize and quiet them. His horse was shot from under him and galloped off, Pitcairn's matched pistols still in their holsters. (They were carried during the rest of the Revolution by General Israel Putnam, Connecticut hero.) Another mount was found for Pitcairn.

Colonel Smith himself was wounded in the leg but stumbled on in spite of it. If they had put him up on a horse, he would have made a splendid target for those native marksmen.

The road behind the British was soon dotted with sprawling uniformed bodies. When those who could walk finally approached Lexington the march became a rout. Order could no longer be maintained. If the relief force sent out by General Gage had not appeared at this moment, surrender of the whole British force would have been inevitable. The war which had not really started would have been over.

Retreat of the British from Concord. An engraving after a painting by Alonzo Chappel.

Lord Percy.

But they did come — a whole brigade. This included three regiments of infantry, a detachment of marines and royal artillery, complete with cannon and an able, experienced young commander, Hugh, Lord Percy.

Percy immediately formed his men into a British square, putting the wounded up front since he feared no fire from the direction of Boston. He had already secured that road with guards and field pieces as he marched along it on his rescue mission.

The rebels continued their random shooting but this new display of force moved them back. They were particularly impressed with the British cannon, especially when one of them sent a ball in one side of the Lexington Meetinghouse and out the other. At that point they took to the more distant ridges and hills and waited for Percy to continue the retreat toward Boston. They seemed to have little desire to attack the troops now massed together in Lexington but preferred a moving target. For one thing they knew the cannon could not be set up while the soldiers were in motion.

This delay in pressing their advantage may have been from lack of leadership, as the fresh militia companies who

Munroe Tavern, Lexington, which served as Percy's headquarters and hospital.

had come in from towns quite far away had not taken part in the previous fighting, and were used to taking orders only from their own officers. Actually, few of the men knew that they had a commanding officer, or, if they did, that he was there. But he was — at least during the closing hours of the British retreat.

Major General William Heath had been appointed hastily by the Committee of Safety in February when the possibility of real conflict was first apparent. This 38-year-old farmer was an ardent student of military history and maneuvers, but somehow not exactly in tune with the unexpected violent action of the day. In fact, he seemed strangely unprepared for it in spite of having attended a meeting of the Committee of Safety in Menotomy the evening before specifically devoted to just such a possibility. Unlike Heath, the rest of the committee was so afraid of possible capture, they spent the night in hiding in a nearby cornfield. But Heath rode quietly home to Roxbury instead. He met several armed British patrols on the way — an unusual event in itself — but apparently thought nothing of it, and calmly went to bed. And, strangely enough, when a messenger awakened him at dawn with the news, instead of rushing to join the minutemen, he instead returned to the Committee in Menotomy where they were concentrating on sending the following message to distant towns:

> To all Friends of American Liberty, let it be known that this morning before break of day, a Brigade of 1000 to 1200 men marched to Lexington. The bearer, Israel Bessel, is charged to alarm the country and all persons are desired to furnish him with fresh horses.[3]

74

Mr. Bessel left Menotomy at 10 A.M., but his horse fell dead at Worcester 36 miles away. Another one was provided immediately, and off he went. He was spelled in New London, and other riders took the news to New York and on down the Coast. It took about six days for it to reach Williamsburg, colonial capital of Virginia, where there was an excited response. (See page 101.)

Dr. Warren, who had ridden out from Boston, met Heath near Menotomy, and together they tried to plan some way to bottle up the British before they reached the shelter of Boston. They were unable, however, to have a strategy meeting of officers — if, indeed, they knew at this time who the officers were. Instead they hastily decided to force the British toward Cambridge, down the road Percy had used on his way out to Lexington that morning.

Heath had had the foresight to have the planking on the bridge from Cambridge to Boston torn up, and now the problem was to make the British go back on the road that led to it. To do so they must block the one to Boston which went via the Neck, and Warren and Heath tried to mass some minutemen across it at the fork where the two roads diverged.

Naturally, the minutemen had no wish to present a solid, visible target to the British sharpshooters, but some 20 or 30 did obey orders and strung themselves across the highway. This was the first rebel force Percy had seen to aim at, and he lost no time setting up his cannon. Before the first blast, though, the militia melted away behind barns and stone walls, and Percy proceeded, unchallenged.

Meanwhile his flankers were following his orders to force their way into any house along the way, and kill any man able to shoot a gun. If they met any resistance, they were to set fire to the house, as much to flush out the rebels as to burn the dwelling. Three houses on the road from Lexington to Menotomy were so treated, and several men were killed, some quite innocent of any rebel action.

An idiot boy, for instance, one of the town charges, who had enjoyed seeing the British troops parade on the Common in Boston, came out of his hut to watch the shooting as it seemed much more exciting than the ordinary military drill. He was shot off his perch on a fence post, and two men in an inn along the road were also shown no mercy. They had been ordered to run for their lives by the landlord, who took to the attic and safety. Instead, the gentlemen decided not to waste the flips they had just ordered at the bar, and were run through by bayonets when the British burst in.

A Lexington citizen named Adams, not exactly stalwart in character, had hidden in his barn, because he thought with that name, he would be unlikely to receive mercy from the enemy. His nine-year-old son led his mother and baby sister to safety, but returned to guard their house and the church silver hidden in it. He bravely confronted the grenadiers as they pushed the door open, but they did not hurt him, and did no looting in his presence. They destroyed the well, however, and set fire to the house on leaving. As soon as they were out of sight, the boy put out the fire with his father's new brew of beer.

* * *

After leaving Lexington, encouraged by the presence of Percy's troops, the British flankers got carried away with killing and looting, to the point where their retreat was slowed down by it. Lieutenant Mackenzie of the Royal Welsh Fusiliers reported later that ". . . many houses were plundered by (our) soldiers . . . By all accounts some soldiers stayed too long in the houses and were killed in the very act of plundering . . ."[4]

In Menotomy, a crippled man, Jason Russell, built a flimsy wooden barricade of shingles in front of his house behind which he hid himself to defend his property. He had hardly settled down when seven Danvers minutemen rushed up, asking for shelter from a group of approaching flankers. They took refuge in the house with other colonists, some of whom ran down and hid in the cellar. In a

Jason Russell house, Arlington.

matter of minutes Russell was bayonetted to death on his doorstep by the flankers. Whereupon the soldiers then attacked the Danvers men from front and rear and killed them, but were stopped by the local inhabitants who thrust their muskets up the cellar stairs and dared the redcoats to come and get them. One of them did to his immediate and final regret. When Russell's wife returned to her house, she found her husband's body and 11 others. The Russell house still stands, a memorial to those 12 men, the only colonial building connected with the British march left in what is now a sprawling suburb of Boston.

All of this violence served to enrage the minutemen, who could hardly contain themselves when they found bodies of their old men or their fellow colonists bayonetted, or saw the redcoats making off with such precious items as chickens, piglets or pewter.

Thus the rebel force that kept following and sniping at the British became more and more determined to stop them. They might indeed have done so if it had not been for the delaying action of a certain Colonel Timothy Pickering who commanded over 300 Salem militia. Other towns north of Boston, like Danvers, had answered the call for minutemen when the messenger arrived about nine that morning, but Pickering figured that, since the fighting at Lexington had started at 6 A.M. it would be over by the time he and his men had marched the 15 miles to Boston.

His fellow citizens did not agree with him, and the selectmen, of which he was one, held a stormy meeting to urge him to get going. This he finally did, and arrived with his considerable force just in time to see the last of the British cross to Charlestown to the protection of the battleship *Somerset*, and safety.

George Washington himself wrote:

> If the retreat had not been as precipitate as it was — and God knows it could not well have been more so — the [British] troops must have surrendered or been totally cut off. For they had not arrived in Charlestown half an hour before a powerful body of men from Marblehead and Salem was at their heels, and if they had happened to be one hour sooner [they would have] inevitably intercepted their retreat.[5]

So, thanks to Mr. Pickering and others who were slow in pulling on their boots and reaching for their arms, Percy had rescued a considerable force and prevented the colonials from capturing a large part of the British army in New England. As it was, a stunning victory was conceded to the militia, one that started a new chapter in history.

The facts are that Percy had come out with 1800 men to add to Smith's 700. They had not looked forward to any real opposition but they had lost:

73 killed

176 wounded

20 missing

What with the constant addition of new minutemen, they had probably faced 3500 to 4000 enemy.

As for "ye rebels," their loss was comparatively small:

49 killed

39 wounded

5 missing

The number is unimportant, however, compared to

A LIST of the Names of the PROVINCIALS who were Killed and Wounded in the late Engagement with His Majesty's Troops at *Concord*, &c.

KILLED.

Of *Lexington*.
* Mr. Robert Munroe,
* Mr. Jonas Parker,
* Mr. Samuel Hadley,
* Mr. Jona⁺ Harrington,
* Mr. Caleb Harrington,
* Mr. Isaac Muzzy,
* Mr. John Brown,
Mr. John Raymond,
Mr. Nathaniel Wyman,
Mr. Jedediah Munroe.

Of *Menotomy*.
Mr. Jason Ruffel,
Mr. Jabez Wyman,
Mr. Jason Winship,

Of *Sudbury*.
Deacon Haynes,
Mr. —— Reed.

Of *Concord*.
Capt. James Miles.

Of *Bedford*.
Capt. Jonathan Willson.

Of *Acton*.
Capt. Davis,
Mr. —— Hosmer,
Mr. James Howard.

Of *Woburn*.
* Mr. Azael Porter,
Mr. Daniel Thompson.

Of *Charlestown*.
Mr. James Miller,
Capt. William Barber's Son.

Of *Brookline*.
Isaac Gardner, Esq;

Of *Cambridge*.
Mr. John Hicks,
Mr. Moses Richardson,
Mr. William Massey.

Of *Medford*.
Mr. Henry Putnam.

Of *Lynn*.
Mr. Abednego Ramsdell,
Mr. Daniel Townsend,
Mr. William Flint,
Mr. Thomas Hadley.

Of *Danvers*.
Mr. Henry Jacobs,
Mr. Samuel Cook,
Mr. Ebenezer Goldthwait,
Mr. George Southwick,
Mr. Benjamin Daland, jun.
Mr. Jotham Webb,
Mr. Perley Putnam.

Of *Salem*.
Mr. Benjamin Peirce.

WOUNDED.

Of *Lexington*.
Mr. John Robbins,
Mr. John Tidd,
Mr. Solomon Peirce,
Mr. Thomas Winship,
Mr. Nathaniel Farmer,
Mr. Joseph Comee,
Mr. Ebenezer Munroe,
Mr. Francis Brown,
Prince Easterbrooks,
  (A Negro Man.

Of *Framingham*.
Mr. —— Hemenway.

Of *Bedford*.
Mr. John Lane.

Of *Woburn*.
Mr. George Reed,
Mr. Jacob Bacon.

Of *Medford*.
Mr. William Polly.

Of *Lynn*.
Mr. Joshua Felt,
Mr. Timothy Munroe.

Of *Danvers*.
Mr. Nathan Putnam,
Mr. Dennis Wallis.

Of *Beverly*.
Mr. Nathaniel Cleaves.

MISSING.

Of *Menotomy*.
Mr. Samuel Frott,
Mr. Seth Ruffell.

Those distinguished with this Mark [*] were killed by the first Fire of the Regulars.

Sold in Queen-Street.

A broadside listing the colonists killed in the battle of Lexington and Concord.

the change that had taken place that day in those who survived. In the dawn's early light, they had been Englishmen
rebelling against the unjust laws that their king had placed
upon them. By the end of the day they had become Americans fighting for their freedom.

This heady feeling quickly passed from man to man
as they fought together, then rapidly from town to town,
from colony to colony up and down the coast. The American Revolution had begun.

Grave of Major John Buttrick, Hill Burying Ground, Concord.

PART THREE

The Prominent Men on Both Sides

Many men are involved in this account even though the action takes only 24 hours. Since their number is large and each played an important part, a list follows explaining their role in the events of the day to help the reader keep them straight.

THE COLONIAL OR REBEL SIDE

SAMUEL ADAMS — one of the most radical men in Boston, A rebel leader, he fled to Lexington with John Hancock and Hancock's fiancée, Dorothy Quincy, to escape capture.

CORPORAL AMOS BARRETT — Concord minuteman, whose simple, human account of the day is a wonderful example of eighteenth century New England prose.

COLONEL JAMES BARRETT — commander of the Concord area militia and owner of the farm where the rebel stores were hidden.

MAJOR JOHN BUTTRICK — the colonial officer who gave the famous order at the North Bridge, "Fire, for God's sake, fire!"

REVEREND JONAS CLARKE — minister and prominent patriot in Lexington in whose house Adams, Hancock and Dorothy Quincy hid. Eliza Clarke was his daughter.

COLONEL WILLIAM CONANT — commander of the Boston militia and the man who started Paul Revere on his famous ride.

ISAAC DAVIS — young captain of the Acton militia and the first to be killed in the Concord battle.

WILLIAM DAWES — a shoemaker and courier for the rebels who set out to spread the alarm by the land route (Boston Neck) in case Revere was captured. They met in Lexington but neither one got to Concord.

WILLIAM DIAMOND — the 16-year-old drummer boy who beat the call-to-arms for the Lexington militia.

REV. WILLIAM EMERSON of Concord — whose accurate, spirited writings and sermons did much for the colonial cause.

JOHN HANCOCK — wealthy Bostonian, who was a prominent colonial figure.

WILLIAM HEATH — Major General in charge of the Massachusetts militia.

LIEUTENANT JOSEPH HOSMER — Concord minuteman whose cry at the North Bridge, "Would ye let them burn our town down?" started the Concord fight. His house still stands in Concord.

DEACON JOHN LARKIN — owner of the horse that Revere rode.

ROBERT NEWMAN — sexton of the Old North Church where the lanterns were hung as signals of the British march.

CAPTAIN JOHN PARKER — leader of the Lexington minutemen.

COLONEL TIMOTHY PICKERING — commander of the Salem militia, who arrived just too late to capture the British forces before they got back to Boston.

DOCTOR SAMUEL PRESCOTT — a young Concord doctor whose romance with a Lexington lady resulted in his meeting Revere and Dawes on their way to alarm the Concord countryside. They were captured but Prescott escaped and finished their job for them.

DOROTHY QUINCY — fiancée of John Hancock.

JOSIAH QUINCY — a Boston lawyer and patriot, who wrote Revolutionary pamphlets and was sent to England to argue the rebel cause.

PAUL REVERE — silversmith and courier for the rebels.

DR. JOSEPH WARREN — a remarkably able and courageous Boston doctor who was in charge of the rebel spy system. One of the great Revolutionary figures.

THE BRITISH SIDE

LIEUTENANT JOHN BARKER — of the King's Own Regiment, who wrote a scornful summary of the day's action.

GENERAL HENRY CLINTON — commander-in-chief of the British forces in America after General Gage.

GENERAL THOMAS GAGE — Royal Governor of the Massachusetts Bay Colony and commander of the British forces. He ordered the march to capture the military stores in Concord but did not participate in it.

85

CAPTAIN WALTER LAURIE — light infantry officer in command of the British in the fighting at Concord bridge.

ENSIGN JEREMY LISTER — 10th Regiment of Foot, wounded at the Concord Bridge, who wrote a graphic description of the retreat.

LIEUTENANT FREDERICK MACKENZIE — of the Royal Welsh Fusiliers whose report of the day's fighting is important, first-hand evidence of "what really happened."

CAPTAIN LAWRENCE PARSONS — British officer in charge of the troops sent to the Barrett farm.

HUGH, LORD PERCY — brilliant young British nobleman and able commander of the troops sent to aid Colonel Smith in the British retreat from Concord.

MAJOR JOHN PITCAIRN — second in command of the British forces at Lexington and Concord under Colonel Smith.

COLONEL FRANCIS SMITH — who botched up the British march by his slowness and indecision. He was commander of the expedition.

LIEUTENANT WILLIAM SUTHERLAND — of the 38th Regiment, another officer who wrote a vivid account of the day's events.

PART FOUR

The Men Who First Wrote About the Lexington and Concord Battles

You who read this book might like to know how the facts about the battles of Lexington and Concord came to be recorded. This story of a story is quite fascinating in itself.

The fighting at Lexington and Concord started the American Revolution. It also inspired a flood of literature on the subject which varies from the first terse depositions (sworn statements) by militiamen, to sermons from the many colonial pulpits, and letters from one officer or official to another. Then came the sifting of evidence, the long-winded arguments, and the heated, conflicting claims between the towns of Arlington*, Concord and Lexington as to where the first action took place.

This was followed by lengthy papers, orations, and literary essays of the nineteenth century, some of them full of misinformation because what one writer said might have

---

* The town of Menotomy (an Indian word meaning swift water) changed its name to Arlington in 1867 in honor of Arlington National Cemetery. Occasional efforts have been made to change it back but so far none has been successful.

happened on one day, the next writer said *did* happen on that day. In this way incidents that did not occur became "facts," and people appeared or disappeared on the scene at the will of historians, essayists, or — in one important instance — a poet. Henry Wadsworth Longfellow, for example, took the events and the characters that appealed to him and made a narrative poem of them. His *Paul Revere's Ride* has been the favorite source of information on the subject for one hundred years even though he omitted such an important man as William Dawes, and had Paul Revere spreading the alarm of the British march in Concord in spite of the fact that he never got there. There are many other historical errors in it but it is still published for children and taken as truth, presumably.

Actually, Longfellow had little excuse for the liberty he took with the events because even during his lifetime (1807-1882) the basic facts were known from the many contemporary writings in existence at that time.

Few important military events have been so promptly documented. Eye-witness reports or depositions were taken by justices of the peace just a few days after the last minute-man put down his smoking musket, and watched the weary British take refuge in Charlestown. It is a measure of the smartness of Sam Adams, Joseph Warren and John Hancock that they realized the importance of the 24 hours that made up April 19, 1775, even before the day was over. Though they were still subjects of George III, the patriot leaders now felt they had proof of his inhumanity.* Their

---

* This explains the emphasis at that time on the claims that the British shot first at both Lexington and Concord. Nowadays we are not so concerned with which side started the fight; the important thing is that it *did* start.

rebellion against his unjust laws and taxes would be justified at last in the eyes of the other colonies and the world. In fact, Adams and Hancock quickly sensed that while they must mourn the deaths of their minutemen, their sacrifice was just what was needed for the rebel cause.

For one thing, the news of the colonial victory would have a wonderfully unifying effect among the colonies. Recent talks about reconciliation with the mother country would now be forgotten. And, best of all, the British boast that the colonists were cowards and would never stand up to the regular British soldiers was proven completely false. In the House of Commons, just two months before Lexington and Concord, Lord Sandwich, a prominent nobleman and head of the Admiralty, addressed the Prime Minister:

> The noble Lord [North] mentions the impracticality of conquering America. I cannot think the noble Lord can be serious on this matter. Suppose the Colonies do abound in men, what does that signify? They are raw, undisciplined, cowardly men. . . . Believe me, the very sound of a cannon would carry them off . . . as fast as their feet could carry them . . .[6]

But the evidence of the unexpected colonial courage, stamina and ability had to be presented in a convincing manner. The leaders must get it in writing. So the Massachusetts Provincial Congress moved quickly to appoint a committee of nine men to take sworn testimony between April 23rd and 25th from everyone involved in the march.

Ninety such depositions were written down word for word and constitute 21 separate documents now stored in the libraries of Harvard College and the University of Virginia. For the most part, they are short, to the point, and

No 11

Lexington April 25, 1775.

I William Draper of lawful age, and an inhabitent of Colrain in the County of Hampshire and Colony of Massachusetts-Bay in New-England do testify and declare, that being on the parade of said Lexington April 19th instant about half an hour before sunrise, the King's regular troops appeared at the meeting house of Lexington. Captain Parker's company, who were drawn up back of said meeting house on the parade turned from said troops making their escape by dispersing. In the mean time the regular troops made an huzza and ran towards Captains Parker's company who were dispersing; and immediately after the huzza was made, the commanding Officer of said troops, (as I took him) gave the command to the said troops, "fire! fire! damn you fire!" and immediately they fired, before any of Captain Parker's company fired. I then being within three or four rods of said regular troops. And further say not.

William Draper

Middlesex ss April 25th 1775

William Draper above Named being duly Caution to Testify the whole Truth made Solemn Oath to the Truth of the above Deposition by him Subscribed

Wm Reed
Coram Josiah Johnson Jus Pac
Wm Stickney

An original deposition by minuteman Draper.

Note: when reading the above, remember that the letter "s" was written " *ſ* " in those days except when "s" was the final letter in a word. *Reprinted by permission of the Harvard College library.*

without emotional exaggeration. In fact, they are much more believable and effective than the florid official report written for the Provincial Congress by its seemingly patriotic but actually traitorous Dr. Benjamin Church.

Church, a prominent doctor and surgeon, was a member of the Provincial Congress, but, more important, he was one of the select Committee of Safety that decided on the whole rebel policy, both political and military. General Gage realized he must learn all plans of this committee and offered substantial bribes to Sam Adams and Church to divulge them. Needless to say, Adams turned him down, but Church accepted and reported regularly to Gage on training, stores, as well as the movements of rebel leaders.

It was probably his information that sent Gage after the Concord stores, but Church's infamy was not proven until the summer of 1775. His final downfall does not bear directly on Lexington and Concord, but it is so fascinating that a summary of it may be found in the footnote below: *

* Church may have tried to salve his guilty conscience by writing over-patriotic reports of rebel achievements for his fellow colonists like his description of the British march on Concord during which he claimed pregnant women were dragged from the houses and innocent farmers were molested. It was a similarly exaggerated account about the great strength of the militia that got him in trouble. After the retreat of the British to Boston, Gage was bottled up there by rebel forces. Church wrote him a letter in cipher and gave it to a lady friend to smuggle in. Instead, the letter fell into the hands of General Greene, one of General Washington's staff, who delivered it to his chief. Church was brought before Washington and his generals and convicted of treason, whereupon an unusual problem presented itself. When the disciplinary code of the new American army was drawn up, no punishment for espionage was included because no one dreamed that it would occur. Church was sentenced to prison in Connecticut, however, "without pen or ink" but was later released to a Massachusetts prison because of ill health. The British General Howe offered to exchange an important colonial prisoner for him; the Massachusetts Congress would not let him go, and eventually he was banished to an island in the West Indies, which was a barbaric wilderness at that time. He left in a "smalle schooner" and was never heard of again.

To return to the depositions, Paul Revere himself wrote two accounts of his famous ride, a brief one in 1783, and a much longer one in a letter to the secretary of the Massachusetts Historical Society in 1798. On page 56 is his description of the start of his trip. Here he tells about his capture:

> We had got nearly halfway [to Concord]. Mr. Dawes and the doctor stopped to alarm the people of a house . . . when I saw two men . . . they being armed with pistols and swords, they forced us into a pasture. The doctor jumped his horse over a stone wall and got to Concord. . . . they ordered me to dismount. The one in command asked me if I was an express. I answered in the affirmative. He demanded what time I left Boston, and I added that their troops had catched aground in . . . the river, and that there would be 500 Americans there in a short time, for I had alarmed the country all the way up. . . . One of the officers, a Major Mitchell of the 5th regiment, clapped his pistol to my head, called me by name, and told me he was going to ask me some questions, and if I did not give him true answers he would blow my brains out.[7]

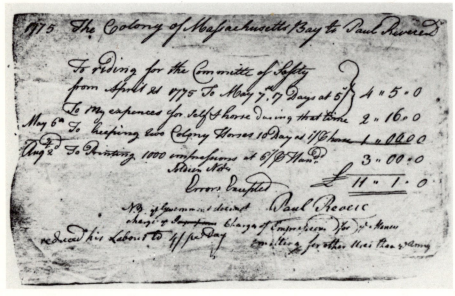

Paul Revere's bill to the Committee of Safety for his services on the night of April 18, 1775.

Granary Burying Ground, Boston. The graves of Samuel Adams, John Hancock, Joseph Warren, Peter Faneuil and Paul Revere are here.

A separate set of depositions was taken from survivors 50 years later in 1825, and others in 1827, and in 1835. These were mostly to honor the aged veterans of that great day, and are to some extent the shaky recollections of old people, but they do add some colorful and plausible details.

Other contemporary accounts are also valuable in this regard, such as those found in personal writings. Fortunately it was fashionable for educated men (and some women) of that era to keep diaries. For instance, one of the most interesting and detailed accounts of the whole day was found in the diary of Lieutenant Frederick Mackenzie

93

of the Royal Welsh Fusiliers. It is excellent, perceptive reporting.

> During the whole of the march from Lexington the Rebels kept an incessant irregular fire from all points at the column [of British troops], which was the more galling as our flanking parties, which at first were placed at sufficient distances to cover the march of it, were at last, from the different obstructions they occasionally met with, obligated to keep almost close to it. Our men had very few opportunities of getting good shots at the Rebels, as they hardly ever fired but under cover of a stone wall, from behind a tree, or out of a house; and the moment they fired they lay down out of sight until they had loaded again or the column had passed. In the road indeed in our rear, they were numerous and came on pretty close, frequently calling out, "King Hancock forever! [8]

Another interesting diary is by the Rev. William Emerson of Concord, grandfather of Ralph Waldo Emerson, who was first to answer, gun in hand, the alarm rung from his church when Dr. Prescott arrived. However, he chose to stay with the older militia or "alarm company" while the minutemen marched off to meet the British on the Lexington Road. His description is typical of the prose of that period:

> . . . To see our aged Sires that morning, whose bended Shoulders had long been freed from martial Labors take Fire again, throwing off the Weight of more than three score years, with quickened Step . . . conquered enffebled Nature, while a short Youth boiled up within their Veins, and strung their Nerves anew . . . [9]

* Except for the above, the spelling, punctuation and capitalization of all original material quoted in this book has been somewhat modernized, as there was no uniform writing style at that time.

Also, with no telephone or telegraph, letter writing was a very important way of sending information, news, or just gossip. In fact, to write a graciously worded but explicit letter in a fine, even script was considered an art by both sexes. And the correspondence of this period often reflected the breeding and staunch character of the writers.

For instance, Eliza Clarke, daughter of the Rev. Jonas Clarke, wrote to her niece on April 19th, 1841, of what she saw 66 years before from her father's house near Lexington Green when she was but 12 years old.

> ...I can see in my mind just as plain all the British troops marching off the (Lexington) Common to Concord, and

Hancock-Clarke house, Lexington.

the whole scene, how Aunt Hancock and Miss Dolly Quincy, with their cloaks and bonnets on, Aunt crying and wringing her hands, and helping Mother dress the children, Dolly going round with Father to hide money, anything down in the potatoes and up garrett.

Father, Mother with me . . . went to the Meeting House where was the eight men killed, all in boxes, made of four large boards nailed up, and after Pa had prayed, they were put into horse carts and took into the grave yard where Grandfather and . . . the neighbors had made a large trench. . . . I saw them let down into the ground . . . and covered up with clods, and then for fear the British should find them, . . . some men cut pine or oak bows and spread them on their place of burial.[10*]

It was also the golden age of oratory at political and cultural meetings, in churches, and at outdoor rallies such as those held under the Liberty Tree. Sam Adams was a loud and persuasive speaker, as was Dr. Church, the spy.

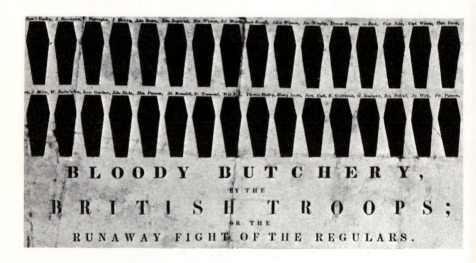

The coffins on this colonial poster represent minutemen killed on April 19.

Rev. Jonas Clarke, father of the letter writer Eliza, and host to Adams and Hancock, gave his version of the entire action in a sermon commemorating the first anniversary of the event. Here is his account of the start of the battle.

> ...The foremost [British officer] who was within a few yards of our men, brandishing his sword, and then pointing towards them, with a loud voice said to the troops, "Fire! by God, fire!" — which was instantly followed by a discharge of arms ...succeeded by a very heavy and close fire upon our party ...as long as any of them were within reach. Eight were left dead upon the ground! Ten were wounded. The rest of the company through divine goodness, were to a miracle preserved unhurt in this murderous action.[11]

Clarke and Emerson were only two of several local ministers who showed no fear in blasting King George and his troops from the pulpit. The Rev. Edward Stiles, then President of Yale College, even took an enthusiastic part in the fighting.

Luckily, many of these speeches and other contemporary writings as well as significant newspaper articles of that time were collected and preserved by a man who realized their unique value even in the early days of our nation. He was Peter Force, (1790-1868) a New Jersey printer who fought in the War of 1812, and later served as Mayor of Washington. He had the noble ambition of assembling all the Revolutionary documents he could lay his hands on, and he did a magnificent job on the years 1774-1776 before his funds ran out. His collection fills nine volumes that are housed in the National Archives — a tremendous boon to all scholars of the period.

Another man, Frank Moore, (1828-1904) son of a
New Hampshire newspaper publisher, made a vital contri-
bution to our storehouse of Revolutionary material. His
Diary of the American Revolution is a compilation of
newspaper articles, broadsides and ballads of the day — a
fascinating collection that was first published in 1860, re-
issued for 15 years and then allowed to go out of print for
one hundred. It is now available in a new edition, published
in 1967, a volume that teems with the heated political opin-
ions of the day, the violent battles, sieges and shifting for-
tunes of the war, as well as the irrepressible and ribald humor
of both the common people and the leaders.

This colonial cartoon portrays the British soldiers as donkey

Benjamin Franklin, no less, composed a poem called *The King's Own Regulars* after the British retreat. It was published in the *Pennsylvania Evening Post*.

> No troops [the British] perform better than we at reviews
> We march and we wheel, and whatever you choose
> George [III] would see how we fight, and we never re-
> fuse . . .
> It was not fair to shoot at us from behind trees
> If they had stood open, as they ought, . . . we should have
> beat them with ease
> They may fight with one another that way if they please
> But it is not *regular* to stand and fight with such rascals
> as these.[12]

ooting and burning as they retreat from Concord.

Franklin was obviously no poet, but his gleeful enjoyment of the situation needs no apology.

Another lighthearted example of public opinion can be found in a popular ballad circulated first in 1775 as a newspaper broadside. It was sung to the tune of *The Irish Washerwoman*. Again, it is about the British retreat:

> How brave you went out with your muskets all bright,
> And thought to be-frighten the folk with the sight;
> But when you got there how they powdered your pums
> And all the way home how they peppered your bums.
> And is it not, honeys, a comical crack
> To be proud in the face and shot in the back? [13]

The newspapers of that day are also lively reading, and like modern ones, quick to use any event for political propaganda. The *Massachusetts Spy*, a Boston patriot sheet that had to move quickly to Worcester to prevent British confiscation, aroused other colonial newspapers with this broadside on May 5, 1775:

> AMERICANS! Forever bear in mind the BATTLE OF LEXINGTON where British Troops, unmolested and unprovoked, wantonly ... killed a number of our countrymen, then ... ransacked, plundered and burned their houses. Nor could the tears of denfenseless women, some in the pains of childbirth, and cries of helpless babies, nor the prayers of old age ... appease their thirst for blood ...! [14]

A Weekly, Political, and Commercial PAPER , open to ALL Parties, but influenced by None.

From the above and from scores of other original documents found in congressional reports, town histories, historical societies, public and private libraries, museums and other institutions, it is possible to learn the American point of view at the time of the Lexington and Concord engagements. It was many-sided but on the whole fairly unanimous along the whole eastern seaboard. Of course, there were many Loyalists, men and women still devotedly British, but they were for the most part out-talked and out-written. A good number left the country.

Here is a typical reaction in the colony of Virginia to the news of the fighting at Lexington and Concord.

> Yesterday there was a meeting at Williamsburg of the committee and militia of King William County when the contents of the express from the northward was communicated. It had such an effect on the minds of the people that near 200 pounds was immediately subscribed for the use of our brethren now fighting in the common cause.[15]

As to the British side of it, the official reports of General Gage, Colonel Smith and Lord Percy were known soon after the fighting. Gage even sent a report to the colonial governors to offset the propaganda that the British had fired first. He naturally played down the whole engagement as insignificant, as indeed it was in size and duration compared to the European campaigns of that time. Percy, however, confessed that his men had been under heavy pressure.

> As soon as they saw us begin to retire, they pressed very much upon our rear guard, which . . . I relieved every now

and then. In this manner we retired for 15 miles under incessant fire all round us, till we arrived at Charlestown between 7 and 8 in the even, very much fatigued...[16]

Percy mentions in this same letter the one atrocity committed by the Americans during that day. A young boy crossed the North Bridge after the fighting, and found a near-dead British soldier on the ground. Unaccountably, he split his head open with a hatchet he was carrying. Captain Parsons, returning from the Barrett farm found him and reported to Percy that the man had been scalped, a statement that was widely circulated.

The British apparently did not know what a proper scalping looked like, nor for that matter did the Americans, as authorities say it had been a hundred years since one had been reported. Without doubt, accusations that flowed from both sides loomed larger at the time than they do from modern historical perspective. As has been said, the American evidence and some of the official British records were known and talked about right away, but it took a century and a half for the whole British point of view to be pieced together.

For instance, Gage's governmental documents were circulated quickly, but his private papers were not found until the late 1920's, collecting dust in the Public Records Office in London. An American philanthropist, William Clements, bought them and they are now in the Clements Library at the University of Michigan.

They contain such priceless items as Major Pitcairn's personal account of the Lexington fight, the report by Captain Laurie, British commander at the Concord bridge, the earlier segment of Lieutenant Mackenzie's diary, which filled in gaps on the start of the British march, and the frequent pay-offs of Benjamin Church. (The diary was published as a whole by the Harvard University Press in 1926 under the title, *A British Fusilier in Colonial Boston*.)

Also found were the papers of General Henry Clinton, who did not participate in the Lexington and Concord events but fought at Bunker Hill and eventually took Gage's place as commander of the British forces in America. Since some of Gage's officers stayed on to serve under

General Gage's pew, Old North Church.

General Clinton, their reports of earlier events found their way into his files. Hence, when the Clinton collection was also acquired by Mr. Clements, a considerable amount of new information became available to scholars interested in the American Revolution in general, and the 24 hours of Lexington-Concord in particular.

For example, a long narrative by Lieutenant William Sutherland of the 38th regiment, who was one of the officers who rode up with Pitcairn to the Lexington Green, supplied previously unknown details of the action although, as one historian said, he was apt to "not exaggerate but multiply" the strength of the enemy. He wrote critically to General Clinton of the start of the expedition say-that the troops, when they landed on the other side of the Charles River, were up to their middles in water, and threw away the rations that were meant to hold them through the day.

Ensign Jeremy Lister of the 10th Regiment of Foot, who was wounded at Concord, also told the whole story of the day in a narrative that was eventually printed by the Harvard University Press in 1931. We learn from him of the agony of his trip back to Boston.

> ...we was then met by a reinforcement of 4 batteries under Lord Percy to our great joy as our ammunition being then nearly expended...This meeting...caused a little halt when I got Mr. Simes, Surgeon's Mate, to examine my arm when he extracted a ball it having gone through the bone... Not having had a morsel since the day before, I begun to grow rather faint, seeing Colonel Smith borrow a horse from an officer of marines, he having been wounded in the leg, I applied to him to lend me his horse, which he did, seeing al-

most immediately a soldier eating a little biscuit and beef I begged to partake with him. He generously complied which was about a mouth full of each. When we proceeded on our march, I begged a grenadier to give me a little water in my hat out of a horse pond which refreshed me a good deal. When I had road about 2 miles I found the balls whistled so smartly about my ears I thought it more prudent to dismount . . . so I went from one side of the horse to the other when a horse was shot dead close by me that had a wounded man on his back and three hanging by his sides . . .[17]

There is also a report from Lieutenant John Barker of the King's Own Regiment who obviously did not approve of Colonel Smith's plans or their execution.

Thus for a few trifling stores the Grenadiers and Light Infantry had a march of about 50 miles through an enemy's country and in all human probability must every man have been cut off if the Brigade (under Lord Percy) had not fortunately come to their assistance.[18]

So there are many original sources, which vary wide-

ly in attitude, literary worth and content. This brief summary does not do them justice, but hopes to lead the interested reader on to his own research.

There are also literally hundreds of volumes written in this century and the last on all aspects of the Revolution — political, religious, economical and sociological. No subject has been more thoroughly explored, but, in this author's opinion, there are certain modern writers and editors who manage to bring its action and its significance closer to the general reader than others.

Sir George Trevelyan's four volume *The American Revolution*, although not up to date in all respects, is still the most comprehensive. Another valuable work is *The Growth Of The American Republic* by Samuel Eliot Morison and Henry Steele Commager (2 vols.). Mr. Commager has also contributed one of the most valuable source books. Richard B. Morris was co-editor with him of *The Spirit of 'Seventy-six*, which has an excellent running commentary and a wide selection of original writings covering all phases of the war including Lexington and Concord. One of the most discerning, accurate and enjoyable books on the events of April 19th, 1775 is William Tourtellot's *William Diamond's Drum*.

There are many bibliographies of the Revolution such as those in the *Harvard Guide to American History*, of which there is a new edition. Most of the books mentioned, though, give little space to Lexington and Concord.

Perhaps the greatest scholar of this particular part of the Revolution was the late Allen French of Concord. His

Day of Concord and Lexington was published in 1925, and hence does not include some of the latest British information, but Mr. French completed his history in 1932 with the publication of *General Gage's Informers*, which does include his appraisal of the newly found original sources. Both are very readable as well as exact in the most scholarly manner.

With all this material available, it is possible to weigh the mass of evidence of what went on during the memorable day. Points of view on some details and some personalities will always differ, and the concerned reader will consider them all. The Americans should not be thought of as sinless patriots nor should the British be painted as heartless villains. Some of them, like so many of our soldiers in Vietnam, were fighting in a foreign land for a cause they did not believe in.

The clouds of doubt, make-believe and half-truths have been mostly swept away, leaving the facts uncovered. They testify that the action at Lexington and Concord was typical of the nation it helped to push into being — simple in purpose, somewhat imperfect in performance, innovative, and above all, courageous.

A British officer, Captain W. G. Evelyn of the King's Own Regiment wrote to his father on April 23, 1775:

> You must hear an account of . . . the little fracas between us and the Yankey scoundrels. . . . The rebels are the most absolute cowards, yet they are worked up to such a degree of enthusiasm, they are persuaded . . . they must be invincible.[19]

And that, in the end, is what they were.

Spring thaw on the Concord River.

Information For Visitors to Lexington and Concord

Note: check visiting hours at the local tourist bureaus

In Arlington, or Menotomy as it was called in the eighteenth century, little is left to mark its part in the stirring events of April 19th. However, the Jason Russell house still stands on the corner of Jason Street and Massachusetts Avenue, and may be viewed from April to October. Its sturdy simplicity is a fitting memorial to the 12 men who died there. Besides this there are various markers that indicate the sites of colonial homes, stores and so on, which might interest Revolutionary War buffs.

Jason Russell house, Arlington.

It is pleasant to travel on to Lexington and Concord, two charming New England towns that have kept their identity and many of their colonial buildings, thanks to far-seeing and determined citizens. Consult a map, as the area may be approached from Rt. 128, the circular expressway around Boston, or by smaller routes to Rt. 2A in Lexington. Start here and pick up the old Battle Road to Concord along which the British marched. It is clearly marked, as are the interesting buildings and sites along it.

In Lexington, the Munroe and Buckman taverns are both beautifully preserved and cared for along with many historic houses like the Rev. Jonas Clarke's. That is just a short way from the famous green, the Meeting House, and a replica of its intriguing freestanding (separate) Belfry Tower. The handsome statue of Captain John Parker, minuteman, dominates the scene, as it should.

Now proceed slowly along Battle Road (Rt. 2A), parts of which can actually be driven over. They are short detours off the main route, their narrow lengths winding through fields and woods that closely resemble the rural scene the British glimpsed going and coming on that famous day. On this road or very near it are several original and beautiful homes like those of Samuel and Job Brooks and the famous Meriam house, built in 1639, that was well over a hundred years old even on that long-ago day. The Minute-man National Historical Park and Headquarters are on this route.

Continue on to Concord where there is much to see. The old battleground has been refurbished into a hand-

Detail of Boston's Old North Church, where signal lights warned of the British march.

Old Manse on the Concord River.

some park, the "rude bridge that arched the flood" (and in spring it really does!) has been rebuilt, and nearby are the graves of two British soldiers who died in the battle. The fine minuteman statue by Daniel Chester French stands here. Near the battlefield is the William Emerson house, the "Old Manse," where Ralph Waldo Emerson and Nathaniel Hawthorne each lived for a time in later years. From its lawn it is said that William Emerson watched the battle, much to the dismay of his wife who thought him in danger. There is a bullet hole from a British musket in a dwelling nearby, that of Elisha Jones, a minuteman.

Near the Common, the Wright Tavern still stands just as it did when the British officers ate breakfast there,

Wright Tavern, Concord.

and the First Parish Church is the site of the First Provincial Congress presided over by John Hancock. Part of the Colonial Inn on the Common was built in the early 18th century and rebel stores were kept here during the Revolution. It was a private home until 1888 when it became a boarding house, and soon after an inn. It has been serving excellent New England food ever since.

There are many more authentic colonial houses, barns and churches that have been lovingly cared for. For anyone who likes eighteenth century architecture, it is worthwhile to tour the nearby highways and back roads at a leisurely pace because, examples of the "real thing" like the homes of Colonel James Barrett and Major John Buttrick, are to be seen at almost every turn.

Home of Major John Buttrick, Concord.

Buy the local guidebooks at the tourist centers, the Inn, or the Concord Bookshop (an excellent one), so you can identify the historical sites and landmarks, and visit the Concord Antiquarian Society's Museum where there is an impressive diorama of the Concord battle as well as one of Paul Revere's lanterns, and other priceless objects and pieces of furniture in beautifully furnished rooms of the period.

Concord is also famous for its nineteenth century cultural past, and there is much tangible evidence of that left, too. Ralph Waldo Emerson, Henry David Thoreau, Nathanial Hawthorne and the Alcotts all lived here. "Orchard House" where *Little Women* was supposedly written, and the "Wayside" rich in tradition of the Alcotts, Hawthorne and Margaret Sidney, may be visited. The "Wayside" was also the home of Captain Whitney, a fifer in the Revolution.

Most nature lovers will want to walk around Walden Pond, immortalized by Thoreau, and perhaps picnic on its shores. The pond is beautiful in any season but best in spring or fall. Lexington and Concord are good places to visit by car. Avoid the weekend crowds, if possible, and come early in the day to Concord because the parking lots fill up quickly.

The main headquarters for the Massachusetts Audubon Society are in the nearby township of Lincoln. Here this organization operates the world-famous Drumlin Farm, which is a 220-acre spread of pasture, fields, woodland and pond areas with all the domestic and wild animals, poultry and birds that would be found in or near such a farm at the turn of the century. There are scheduled pro-

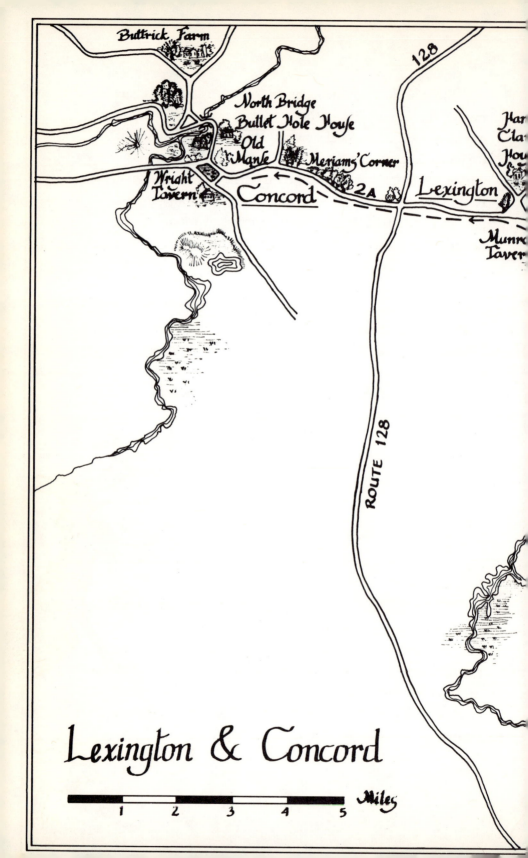

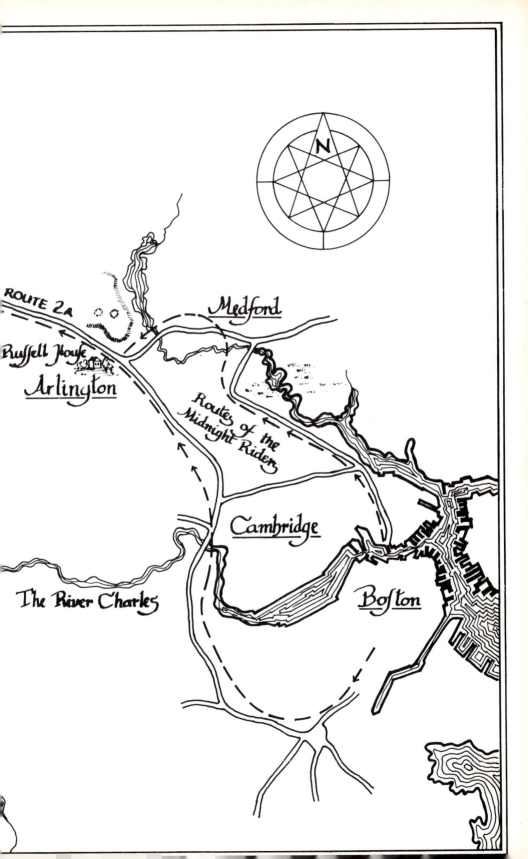

grams for school children, but families can tour the place to the delight and education of young and old.

A stop at Drumlin Farm makes a rather nice change of pace if you have been "doing" history rather heavily in and around Boston. Another delightful switch is a visit to the DeCordova Museum in Lincoln. A successful tea broker, investor and art collector, Julian DeCordova bequeathed his Lincoln estate to the town of Lincoln in 1929, for use as a public museum and park. Now organized as a non-profit organization, this museum has an extensive exhibition program that brings art from all parts of the world, with an emphasis on contemporary work in painting, sculpture, graphics, crafts, architecture and photography. There are classes in these arts for adults and children as well as concerts, lectures, and workshop demonstrations. Call to see what is scheduled on the day of your visit.

*　*　*

To return to Lexington and Concord, those who like to see history recreated can come on any April 19th and watch "Dr. Prescott" canter down the road in the early hours. Then later on in the day there are mock battles with cannon firing, minutemen and grenadiers marching in uniform, fife and drum corps tooting and drumming, and hundreds of visitors cheering them on. All of which is fun to view, especially for children, but peaceful, everyday Lexington and Concord have an atmosphere of their own as do the winding roads that lead to both towns. They are typical of rural New England at its best.

NOTES

1. Revere, Deposition, Massachusetts Historical Society Proceedings XVI, pp. 371.
   Commager and Morris, eds., *The Spirit of '76*, p. 69.
2. *Ibid.*
3. Ward, *The War of the Revolution*, Vol. I, p. 52.
4. Mackenzie, Diary, Mackenzie Papers, Vol. C, p. 43.
   Commager and Morris, p. 87.
5. Sparks, ed., *Correspondence of the American Revolution*, Vol. II, p. 407.
   Tourtellot, *William Diamond's Drum*, p. 202.
6. Earl of Sandwich, *Private Papers of the Earl of Sandwich*, Barnes and Owen, ed., I. p. 63.
   Commager and Morris, p. 97.
7. Revere, p. 371.
8. Mackenzie, p. 20.
9. Emerson, "Diary," French, *Day of Concord and Lexington*, p. 158.
10. Tourtellot, p. 143.
11. Hudson, *History of the Town of Lexington*, p. 530.
12. Franklin, "The King's Own Regulars," *Pennsylvania Evening Post*, March 30, 1776.
    Moore, comp. *Diary of the American Revolution*, p. 106.
13. Moore, p. 27.
14. *Ibid.*, p. 20.
15. Crozier, "Letter to Dr. Rogers," *William and Mary Quarterly*, Jan. 1953, p. 107.
    Commager and Morris, p. 88.
16. Percy, *Letters*, Bolton, ed., p. 51.
    Commager and Morris, p. 88.
17. Lister, "Concord Fight," *The Nineteenth of April, 1775*, Sawtell, ed., p. 30.
18. Barker, "Diary of a British Officer," *Atlantic Monthly* XXXIX, 1877.
    Commager and Morris, p. 74.
19. Evelyn, *Memoirs and Letters*, Scull, ed., p. 89.

AUTHOR'S
ACKNOWLEDGMENTS

I am grateful to many people for their help with this book. These include Mr. Leo Flaherty of the Massachusetts State Archives; Miss Winifred Collins of the Massachusetts Historical Society; Mr. W. H. Bond of the Houghton Library, Harvard University; Miss Arlene Kleeb of the Clements Library, University of Michigan; Miss Cynthia Kriston, of the National Minutemen Park, Lincoln; Father Ancrum of the Old North Church and Mr. Mostone, Sexton; Mrs. Barker, Mrs. Moss and Mrs. Harris of the Concord Public Library; Mrs. Gshwendtner at the Buckman Tavern, Lexington; Mrs. Roberts at the Hancock-Clarke House, Lexington; Mrs. Munroe at the Munroe Tavern, Lexington, and Mr. Lawrence Whipple of Lexington; also Mrs. O'Day of the Arlington Public Library and Mrs. Marjorie Cole of the Concord Bookshop.

I especially appreciate the careful reading of the book in manuscript form by Mr. Laurence Richardson and Mrs. Edmund Fenn of Concord, Mr. William McCullum and Mrs. Daniel Sangster of Duxbury. I wish to give a special note of gratitude to my many varying but always persistent editors: Judy Donnelly, Verna Bayley, Joan Butler and Susan Thaler.

SOURCES OF ILLUSTRATIONS

Antique Views of the Town of Boston, James H. Stark, 1888, page 15 (top), 21, 22, 24, 28, 32-33, 49, 56, 59, 61, 66-67; Arlington Historical Society, 77; Bedford Public Library, Print Department, 20, 31, 34; Boston State House, 38; John Carter Brown Library, Brown University, 29, 68-69, 80, 98-99; *Bunker Hill Memorial Tablets* 1889, 40-41; Concord Antiquarian Society, 23 (top), 48 (photo by Keith Martin); William C. Cousins Collection, 39; Daughters of the American Revolution Museum, 30 (on loan to the DAR Museum, Washington, D.C., from the Boston Tea Party Chapter (272.22); Emmett Collection, New York Public Library, 18; Harvard College Library, 90; *A History of Boston*, Caleb H. Snow, 1825, 15 (bottom); *History of the Siege of Boston*, Richard Frothingham, 1873, 46; *An Impartial View of the Present War in America*, The Rev. James Murray, London, 1780, 26, 35 (right); Kinnaird, Clark, 6, 16, 71; Lawrence Memorial Library, Pepperell, 63; Lexington Historical Society, 51, 54, 70, 96; Library of Congress, 17, 19; *The Memorial History of Boston*, Justin Winsor, Boston, 1881, 14 (top), 72, 105; Museum of Fine Arts, Boston, 12, 14, 44; *New England Magazine*, 1902, 92; *Old Landmarks and Historic Personages of Boston*, Samuel Adams Drake, Boston, 1876, 23, 81; *Outline of the Life and Works of Colonel Paul Revere*, Towle Manufacturing Company, 1901, 36; *The True Story of Paul Revere*, Charles Gettemy, Boston, 1905, 35 (left).

Maps on pages 10, 52, 116-117 by Yorgis Toufexis.

Photos by Barbara Cooney: Jacket, pages 2, 25, 27, 28, 38, 39, 45, 53, 57, 59, 62, 63, 65, 73, 77, 82, 93, 95, 103, 108, 109, 111, 112, 113, 114.

BIBLIOGRAPHY

Alden, John R. *The American Revolution, 1775-1783*. New York: Harper, 1954.

———. *General Gage In America*. Baton Rouge: Louisiana State University Press, 1948.

Barker, Lieutenant John. "Diary of a British Officer." *Atlantic Monthly* XXXIX. April — May, 1877. Also in *The British in Boston*. Elizabeth Dana, ed. Boston: Little, 1924.

Bailyn, Bernard, ed. *Pamphlets Of The American Revolution, Vol. I*. Cambridge: Harvard University Press, 1965.

Barrett, Corporal Amos. "The Concord and Lexington Battle." *Journal and Letters*, Henry True, ed., Ohio: n.p. 1906.

Beach, Stewart. *Lexington and Concord in Color*. Photographs by Samuel Chamberlain. New York: Hastings, 1970.

Bowen, Catherine D. *John Adams and the American Revolution*. Boston: Little, 1950.

Centennial Celebration of the Concord Fight. Vols. I & II. Concord: Concord Antiquarian Society, 1876.

Clarke, Rev. Jonas. "The Fate of Bloodthirsty Oppressors." Charles Hudson. *History of the Town of Lexington*. Vol. I. Boston: Houghton, 1913.

Coburn, Frank W. *The Battle of April 19, 1775*. Lexington: 1912.

Commager, Henry S. and Morris, Richard B., eds. *The Spirit of '76*. New York: Harper, 1967.

Crozier, John. "Letter to Dr. Rogers." *Account of Lexington*. J. Tyler, ed. *William and Mary Quarterly*, 3rd series, X, No. 1. January, 1953. Also in Commager and Morris, *The Spirit of '76*.

Cullen, M. R., Jr. *The Battle Road*. Greenwich: Chatham Press, 1970.

de Berniere, Ensign Henry. Narrative, 1775. Massachusetts Historical Society Collections IV.

Draper, W. C. Deposition. Harvard College Library. Houghton American Manuscript Collection. 811.

Emerson, Rev. William. "Diary." Ralph Waldo Emerson. *Miscellanies*. Boston: Houghton, 1893. Also in *Centennial Celebra-*

tion of the Concord Fight and Allen French, *Day of Concord and Lexington.*

Evelyn, Captain W. G. *Memoirs and Letters.* G. D. Scull, ed. Oxford: Parker, 1879. Also in Commager and Morris, *The Spirit of '76.*

Forbes, Esther. *Paul Revere and the World He Lived In.* Boston: Houghton, 1941.

Force, Peter, comp. Documentary History of the English Colonies, 1774-1776. Washington, National Archives, IV Series.

French, Allen. *Day of Concord and Lexington.* Boston: Little, 1925.

———. *General Gage's Informers.* Ann Arbor: University of Michigan, 1968.

Gage, General Thomas. *Correspondence.* E. Clarence, ed. New Haven: Yale University, 1931.

———. Clements Library. Ann Arbor: University of Michigan. a) American Series. b) English Series. c) Mackenzie Papers. d) British Army in America. e) Baldwin Papers (Lexington Selectmen's Reports). f) General Clinton Papers. g) Battle of Lexington Collection — 20 Depositions.

Galvin, Major James R. *The Minute Men (1645-1775).* New York: Hawthorn, 1963.

Gordon, Rev. William. Letter to a Friend in England, May 17, 1775. Peter Force, comp. American Archives. 4th Series II. Also in Harold Murdock, *The Nineteenth of April, 1775.*

Heath, General William. Memoirs. Boston, 1798. Massachusetts Historical Society Collection IV. Also in W. Abbatt, ed. *Memoirs of General W. Heath.* New York: Abbatt, 1901.

Higginbotham, Donald. *The War of American Independence.* New York: Macmillan, 1971.

Hudson, Charles. *History of the Town of Lexington.* Vol. I. Boston: Houghton, 1913. Also in Lexington Historical Society, n.d.

Lancaster, Bruce. *The American Heritage Book of the Revolution.* R. M. Ketchum, ed. New York: Simon, 1958.

———. *From Lexington to Liberty.* Garden City: Doubleday, 1955.

Lister, Ensign Jeremy. *Concord Fight*. Cambridge: Harvard, 1931. Also in Clinton Collection, Clements Library. Ann Arbor, Michigan.

Mackenzie, Lieutenant Frederick. *Diary*. 2 vols. Cambridge: Harvard, 1930. Also in Mackenzie Papers, Clements Library, Ann Arbor, Michigan.

Massachusetts Spy. Worcester, May 3, 1775.

Moore, Frank, comp. *Diary of the American Revolution*. New York: Scribners, 1856. Reprint: New York, Washington Square Press, 1967.

Murdock, Harold. *The Nineteenth of April, 1775*. Boston: Houghton, 1923.

Percy, Hugh, Earl. *Letters*. C. H. Bolton, ed. Boston: Goodspeed, 1902. Also in Commager and Morris, *The Spirit of '76*.

Pitcairn, Major John. Report. *Private Papers of the Earl of Sandwich, 1771-1782*. G. H. Barnes and J. H. Owen, eds. London: Navy Records Society, 1907. Also in Gage Papers, Clements Library, Ann Arbor, Michigan.

Pope, Richard. "Report by a Tory Volunteer." *Late News*. Boston: Club of Odd Volumes, 1927.

Rankin, Hugh. *The American Revolution*. New York: Putnam, 1964.

Revere, Paul. Depositions. Account 1, 1783. Account 2, 1798. Massachusetts Historical Society Proceedings XVI.

Russell, Francis. *Lexington, Concord and Bunker Hill*. New York: American Heritage, 1963.

Salem Gazette. Salem, April 21, 1775.

Sandwich, John Montagu, Earl. *Private Papers*. G. H. Barnes and J. H. Owens, eds. London: Navy Records Society, 1907. Also in Commager and Morris, *The Spirit of '76*.

Sawtell, C. C. ed. *The Nineteenth of April, 1775*. Lincoln: Sawtells, 1968.

Shattuck, Lemuel. *A History of the Town of Concord*. Boston, 1835.

Scheer, George and Rankin, H. F. *Rebels and Redcoats*. New York: World, 1957.

Smith, Lieutenant Colonel Francis. First Report. Massachusetts Historical Society Proceedings XIV. Later Report. Allen French, *General Gage's Informers.*

Sparks, Jared, ed., Correspondence of the American Revolution. Boston: Little, 1953.

Sutherland, Lieutenant William. Two Letters. 1) to General Clinton, April 24, 1775. 2) to General Gage, April 25, 1775. Clements Library, Ann Arbor, Michigan. Also in Allen French, *General Gage's Informers.*

Trevelyan, Sir George. *The American Revolution.* Vol. I. New York: Century, 1899.

Tourtellot, Arthur B. *William Diamond's Drum.* New York: Doubleday, 1959.

Ward, Christopher. *The War of the Revolution.* Vol. I. New York: Macmillan, 1952.

Washington, General George. Writings of Washington. Harvard College Library. Houghton Collection. Also in *Correspondence of the American Revolution*, Jared Sparks, ed. Boston: Little, 1953.

INDEX